A young man's search for love

DY/NG

†O

L/VE

ORPHA JAKE'S

Robert J. Yoder

ISBN: 978-0-9847281-0-8

For Additonal Copies Contact:
R.J. Enterprises
Post Office Box 132
Berlin, OH 44610
rudyingtolive2@aol.com

Carlisle Printing
OF WALNUT CREEK LTD
800.927.4196 · carlisleprinting.com
Sugarcreek, Ohio 44681

DEDICATION

Dedicated in loving memory to my dad

JACOB A. YODER

(08-07-1917 – 11-22-1971)

whose prayers for his son were answered in a most unexpected way,

and who must have loved me more than I ever realized.

TABLE OF CONTENTS

01. Jake 1

02. The Boa Constrictor 17

03. Eve 35

04. God's Fabric 41

05. Arrested 47

06. Love 57

07. The Heart 65

08. The Author 73

09. Faith 81

10. Prayer 91

11. Dying To Live 99

About The Cover 107

Acknowledgments 109

About The Author 111

CHAPTER 1

Jake

The sled riding accident was so typical of my childhood. I was constantly collecting cuts and bruises, breaking a bone, and on one occasion, ripping open a gash on my knee so deep that it exposed my knee cap.

One winter, it was a sledding accident. Our neighbors had a beautiful sled-riding hill. We used the terrace at the bottom of the hill as our ramp, launching from there and soaring through the air. On one winter day, the snow was just right, the sun was out, and the neighbor kids were having a great time together, riding down the track of snow and flying over the ramp.

That night was cold; and while we slept, the snow that had slightly melted in the sun during the day froze, making the downhill path something like an Olympic sledding track—sheer ice.

The next morning I was up bright and early. Eager to have the ride of my life, I trudged all alone to the very top of the hill. I put the sled down and away I went, not recognizing the danger that lay ahead. Once I started, there was no stopping.

I was going too fast, and my pleasure quickly turned to fear. I hung on, just hoping I would somehow get through this. Hitting the ramp, I went airborne as the sled started to turn sideways. The sled and I both landed, my wrist under the runner. Luckily, I came through that ride with only a broken arm.

Little did I realize that my life would soon be very much like that sled ride, hurtling downward and out of control.

On a bright, sunny spring day, the fresh smell of new life was bursting forth, grass turned brown by the harsh winter was now green, women were hanging out wash, and farmers were turning soil and getting ready to plant spring crops.

As I drove to my hometown of Walnut Creek, the memories were too real and tears started to flow. I could hardly see to drive. Yes, I wished I had my dad right there beside me so that I could ask him questions about the Bible and we could discuss the Word of God, which was so dear to him. I still miss him.

I miss the little town with the grain elevator where we used to bring the wagon filled with grain to grind into feed. Horrisberger Implement is gone, and now there is the Carlisle Inn. Fire destroyed Schlabach's Store, and today there's a library and a new museum. The little dairy treat where we'd stop after school for the best ice cream this side of the Mississippi has been replaced by a post office. Another little ice cream stop became what is now known as Der Dutchman Restaurant. Mom and Dad once owned a house on the town square, and my brother James lived there when he married; now a doctor's office sits on that spot.

The school I attended for eight years still stands. I'd walk a mile to school, through the fields with our neighbors, the Masts. Junior Mast and I were the same age and in the same grade. We were together so much as little boys that we were almost like brothers.

The circus came to town one day and the tent went up on the school grounds. Both Junior and I knew we would not be allowed to see the show, but we managed to find an excuse to head to town that evening, probably saying we were going to buy an ice cream cone. Instead of going into the tent and risk someone seeing us, we peeked under the canvas and watched the circus acts. The clowns, the elephants, and the show girls in tight outfits were all very fascinating for two little Amish boys.

I grew up on a small, fifty-five acre farm, the youngest of four boys with one older sister and three younger sisters. Yes, there were eight of us.

On the farm, there were cows to milk, chickens, horses, and pigs to feed, wheat and oats to thresh, and corn to pick. I have many fond and wonderful memories of growing up on the farm. We worked hard, but we also rode bicycles (and anything with wheels), swung from our big spruce in the back yard, and kept an assortment of pets—goats, a fox, and crows that actually talked.

In the Amish community where I grew up, feelings of love and affection are not often expressed in words but in action, in deeds of kindness and friendship—like helping a neighbor in need or sharing recipes or inviting someone for a meal.

There was one day that Dad expressed his love for family, his love of the outdoors, and his desire to just have fun. It was an expression of love we children will probably never forget.

It was a blustery winter day, with blowing snow making the roads unfit to drive. We kids were in the mood to go sledding, but we needed a toboggan. We knew that Mom and Dad didn't really have the money to buy a new toboggan, and besides, the stores were all closed.

But Dad was determined that we would have a day of fun in the snow. He took off in the car, drove to Millersburg, and somehow talked the owner of Jane and Sandy's to open the doors so that Dad could buy our toboggan.

We had fun riding down the hill behind our barn, with Dad on the tractor pulling us back up to the top of the hill. But the memory that lingers in my mind to this day is the expression of love that Dad showed for his family. I have kept that toboggan as a memorial and as a symbol of the man I remember as my dad.

Dad developed a heart condition at a young age, a result of a bout with rheumatic fever. Even though his heart was not in very good shape, he did the farming with the help of us boys, worked away as a painter, plus fulfilled the duties of the ministry—all the time, knowing that he could die at any moment. Raising eight children is not an easy task for healthy people, yet Mom and Dad did it, even under the shadow of his poor health.

I remember one time in particular that Dad had a stroke during the night. Mom came upstairs and woke us, telling us to come downstairs; something was wrong with Dad. He was sitting up in bed and looked at us but couldn't say anything, which was very scary to me. Mom told us to kneel by the bed and pray. Eli Mast, our neighbor, came over, the doctor arrived, and by late morning Dad's speech was coming back. He seemed to recover and things went back to normal, but every so often he would have a spell that laid him up for a while.

A bachelor lived in a small house in our woods. When the house was moved to another location, Dad decided to build a cabin where the house had been. He wanted a place where he could be all by himself to study and meditate on the word of God. Dad spent many hours at that cabin in communion with God. People far and wide heard Dad's messages expounding the plan of salvation and new birth through Jesus Christ.

Dad was known among the business people he dealt with, preachers and leaders in the church, and the everyday working man. Even though people didn't always agree with him, they usually respected him. To this day, if you mention the name "Orpha Jake" among the Amish and Conservative community in Holmes County, people will remember the man who was my dad.

I remember a home missionary who was a frequent guest at our house; he always wore a Salvation Army-style hat that read "Moyer Home Missions". There was an Amish homeless man called "Slow Johnny" who had some peculiar ways, but he knew he could always get a bed and a meal at the Yoder house. There were many other visitors at our house, and sometimes preachers stayed and discussed doctrine and theology from the Word of God until the wee hours of the morn. This was all very interesting for me as a young boy, and I would sit on the stair steps in rapt attention, trying to comprehend what it all meant.

Dad wasn't known for a great mind like Einstein or Newton or great wealth like Rockefeller or Warren Buffet. No, Dad was known for the faith that was born in him through the saving power of Jesus Christ. I once wrote this, in reflecting on Dad's life and faith.

My Dad
He wasn't well known
As some men are
Like presidents and movie stars
What really mattered
To him you know,
Was God, the Bible
And the love you show
Many were the trials
He had to face
It was God not men
Who showed him grace

Dad's faith grew because of his desire to know Christ and the power of His resurrection, not only the resurrection of the body, but the resurrection that brought a new life with Christ here and now on this earth. His faith moved him to preach the plan of salvation and the new birth, messages that came from the love Jesus had planted in his heart.

Dad's faith compelled him to stand against the tide of the ritualistic culture that he grew up with in the Amish church and helped him live out his conviction to pray from his heart instead of reading the customary prayers from a book. His faith caused him to lose friendships, but he gained new ones. His faith moved him to help people in need and open his home to strangers. His faith gave him an enduring hope not only in this life, but in the life that is to come.

Dad didn't believe in eternal security, the doctrine that says that once you are saved, you are always saved. He didn't believe that once you accepted Christ as your Savior, you received the keys to heaven and then you did good works to earn your rewards. No, it took faith in Jesus Christ to save you from your sins and to keep you saved by the power of Jesus Christ living in you.

As I grew up and watched my brothers and sisters getting married and having homes of their own, I felt an ache inside me. I wanted to have a wife and a family and a home of my own. I wanted children to play with and a wife who loved me. I even had plans for the house I was going to build. I saw it all as such a pretty picture. Little did I know how long it would be before that dream could become reality.

At our church, we were not permitted to date until we

were eighteen. At a youth convention at our local high school, I got up enough nerve to ask a girl out. We started dating and eventually I fell in love. I wanted to get married, but she wasn't ready to make that step and one night she told me she had decided we shouldn't see each other anymore.

I was devastated and tried to analyze what went wrong. I guessed she just didn't love me the way I loved her. I remember even contemplating running my car off the road and killing myself.

My life had more stress besides the broken heart. The brick plant where I worked required hard labor, and we were putting in extra hours. Then every evening I attended our church's revival meetings. It was all too much for an eighteen-year-old boy. Walking off the job one day, I decided to get away from it all. I needed the warm rays of the sun and the sand of Siesta Key beach to heal my depressed mind.

Without telling Mom and Dad or anyone else, I decided to book my first plane ride. I visited a travel agent in Dover and asked if she could book me on a flight to Sarasota, Florida, that very same day. Driving to Cleveland and boarding an airplane was an entirely new experience for me.

As we flew through severe thunderstorms all the way from Cleveland to Atlanta, I felt like Jonah in the whale, running away from all my problems. The plane dipped and rocked so much that the stewardess had to kneel in the aisle while serving drinks. I ordered a little bottle of whiskey to calm my nerves.

We finally landed at Atlanta, only to learn that our plane to Sarasota was broken down and we had to wait for another plane. Finally arriving at the small Bradenton airport at 4 a.m., I slept at the terminal until morning and then took a shuttle to Pinecraft where my aunt and uncle lived. I called Mom right away and told her where I was.

The warm sun and sand of Florida worked its healing magic. I did not kill myself and I would not die of a broken heart. No, I would just guard my heart from ever being broken again.

I dated a few Conservative Mennonite girls, but none of the relationships lasted. Something always seemed to break us apart.

Between the ages of ten to fifteen, I began to doubt whether there really was a God. Even if there was, I reasoned, I didn't really need Him in my life because I had a brain and physical abilities and I could run my own life. I thought church was just a religion and that it didn't really mean anything.

But in church one Sunday night, the Spirit of conviction was on me as the preacher was preaching; and when the invitation was given, I went forward and accepted Christ as my Savior.

I was sixteen. I would try to live a Christian life, but there were many failures and many ups and downs.

In 1970, Mom and Dad had public auction on September 5, sold the farm, and moved to town. They kept the cabin in the woods, and it wasn't far from our house in town.

Soon after we moved from the farm, I bought a quarter horse. It wasn't long before some of the girls in town were interested in riding and talked their parents into buying them horses. We soon started our own horse club, and there I was, the only guy with a bunch of girls. The girls were not Conservative girls; and as you can imagine, Dad was not thrilled about the whole thing. We even used the cabin for our club meetings, and Mom and Dad probably felt we were desecrating the retreat that had been created for a special spiritual purpose.

I was becoming more and more dissatisfied with the

church's emphasis on rules and regulations and with preachers trying to keep the young people from adapting to worldly ways. Finally, everything came to a head and I was excommunicated from my parents' church. After that, I started attending a local Mennonite church where the pastor was someone I knew and respected.

On the week of Nov 17, 1971, Mom and Dad, Eli and Anna Mast, and Yost Millers went to Grove City, Minnesota, for a minister ordination service. My dad preached on Saturday evening on Isaiah 52:7.

> *How beautiful on the mountains*
> *are the feet of those who bring good news,*
> *who proclaim peace,*
> *who bring good tidings,*
> *who proclaim salvation,*
> *who say to Zion,*
> *"Your God reigns!"*

This would be my dad's last message here on this earth. That night at the home of Alvin Helmuth, Dad suffered a severe stroke. He passed away early Monday morning, November 22, 1971, at University Hospital in Minneapolis, Minnesota. I was twenty-two years old.

As I look back on Dad's life, it's his faith in God his Creator and Jesus Christ his Savior that I remember most. After all these years, I still miss him because of what that faith and love has come to mean to me in my own life.

I remember we children sometimes talked about which one of us Dad liked most. There were some heated arguments about which child was the favored one. Usually I kept silent during these discussions, since I knew I was a disappointment to my dad. One day Dad was so disgusted with me that he told me he didn't think I would ever amount to anything.

We had left the Amish church when I was ten years old and were attending Bethel Fellowship, an Amish-Mennonite church that permitted cars, electricity, and phones. My dad was a minister at this church.

One year, a number of people in the congregation put big, blue gospel signs about four feet square on their barns or shops. Dad put one of those signs on the front of our chicken house. Its big letters read, "PREPARE TO MEET THY GOD." Everyone saw it when they drove into our driveway.

I was around fourteen at the time, and I was embarrassed by that sign. To me, it was something that just didn't fit in and made us stand out in the community. One day when Dad was not at home, I tore down the sign. You can imagine the disappointment on my dad's face when he found out I was the guilty person.

There was a time I felt in my heart that Dad didn't really love me, yet his love followed me throughout life and reached me even after his death. I would discover that only after much heartache and walking very close to the precipice of hell.

CHAPTER 2

The Boa Constrictor

I'm reluctant to face the memories of the next part of my life, unwilling to describe the course my life now took. I'd much rather that no one—especially my grandchildren and future generations—would know these details of my life.

I look at Mark Sanford and Tiger Woods, two recent cases of infidelity, and see their worlds turned upside down. What was hidden has come to light for all the world to see. We can't really hide anything; one day everything will be exposed. Sometimes it does not happen in this life, but everything will come to light at the judgment. Jesus said in Matthew 10:26, "There is nothing concealed that will not be disclosed, or hidden that will not be made known."

I've often said that man left to his own devices will destroy himself. You might say that there are a lot of good people in the world. I am sixty years old, and I can truly say that I have not met too many really bad people in my lifetime. But that doesn't erase the fact that we are all born into sin.

I wouldn't say that man is inherently good or evil. I think that part of it has to do with how we're brought up and what kind of values we are taught. My point here is that most people want to live a good life, but every human being faces the struggle between right and wrong, between good and evil.

Some people do good things out of selfish motives, and some people do good because the law says so and they don't want to get in trouble. Some people just want to fit into society and not be an oddball, so they do what everyone else is doing.

But no matter how hard we try, we all battle with some sin, whether it is greed, pride, selfishness, jealousy, hatred, unforgiveness, lust, or whatever it might be. So this is the state of the human condition, in that we are born in sin and no matter how good a life we live, it is not good enough for God.

Ah, but God's great love for us took care of that. We can be restored to a relationship with the God who created us and loved us so much "that he gave his one and only Son, that whoever believes in him shall not perish but have eternal life" (John 3:16).

Luke tell us in his gospel that when Jesus went to pray in the Garden of Gethsemane before His crucifixion, He was "in anguish" (Luke 22:44). What was Jesus going through that an angel from heaven must come to strengthen Him and that His sweat was like drops of blood falling to the ground? He asked His heavenly Father, "...if you are willing, take this cup from me" (Luke 22:42). Was it the anguish of the death He was facing on the cross or was it something else that was creating this agony? What was in that cup that was so horrible, so distasteful, and causing such pain in His heart?

Jesus was facing something that no other human has ever faced. The cup presented to Him that night in the garden contained all the sins of humanity and all the misery, suffering, death, and anguish that those sins have brought. Jesus Christ, the Son of God, saw all the evil, murder, and corruption from the beginning of time to the end of the world, and it would all be put on one person—and that person was Himself.

How many drops of blood were shed for me
In the Garden of Gethsemane
You saw my sin and looked into hell
In the Garden of Gethsemane

I came to do my Father's will
In the Garden of Gethsemane
Not my will but thine be done
In the Garden of Gethsemane

Show me my own sin
In the Garden of Gethsemane
That leads to Calvary
In the Garden of Gethsemane
---RJY

Yes, He saw me and you in all our wretchedness. Christ had always been connected to His heavenly Father, from whence He had come and where He belonged. Yet here He was, looking into the awful face of sin and all its consequences; and it was almost more than He could bear.

He was without spot or blemish, and yet this was His mission. He knew this was why He had come—to take the sins of the whole world upon Himself and die so that you and I could be set free.

Paul talks about the law of sin and death, and it's much like the law of gravity that decrees if you jump off the Empire State Building and hit the ground, you will die. Even though we might want to blame God or other people for the misery and suffering in the world, every evil thing that has ever happened from the beginning of time until now is caused by sin. Because of sin, there will be judgment, and judgment is ultimately separation from God.

It is only when we recognize sin as the problem in our lives that we can be set free from sin. If you jump from the Empire State Building, wouldn't it be great if Superman swooped in and caught you in his arms and saved you from death? Well, my friends, God did just that in sending His own son Jesus Christ to die on the cross for your sins, to take them away "as far as the east is from the west, so far has he removed our transgressions from us" (Ps. 103:12).

When Jesus was hanging on the cross, He said, "My God, my God, why have you forsaken me?" (Matt. 27:46) Yes, Jesus took my place on that cross so that my punishment would not be separation from God. He took my sins upon himself and all I have to do is recognize my sinful state. I must come to the point in my life that I know I am not good enough—and will *never* be good enough—to stand in the presence of a holy and awesome God. I must see myself for what I really am, as described in Revelations 3:17-18.

> *You say, 'I am rich; I have acquired wealth and do not need a thing.' But you do not realize that you are wretched, pitiful, poor, blind and naked.*
> *I counsel you to buy from me gold refined in the fire, so you can become rich; and white clothes to wear, so you can cover your nakedness; and salve to put on your eyes, so you can see.*

Then I can receive this great gift of love, the greatest gift the world has ever known. The greatest treasure we can ever find in this life is Jesus Christ, who will forgive our sins and come live in our hearts.

Nicky Cruz, a leader of one of the most violent gangs in New York City, came face to face with Dave Wilkerson, a country preacher called by God to preach on the streets of New York. Nicky threatened to kill Dave, but Dave replied that even if he were cut up into a thousand pieces, every piece would still cry out, "Jesus loves you." Today, Nicky is preaching about the love of Jesus Christ and about the transformation of his life by the power of God.

You see, Jesus didn't come to reform but to transform,

which means to change from something old to something new. He came to change the heart of man, to give us new desires, new attitudes, a new life in Jesus Christ. He came to restore our relationship with God that was broken because of sin.

Long ago in the garden, Jesus saw all my sins. And he took my punishment for what I've done. For you to get a picture of how we become ensnared by the power of sin and to show the power of Christ and His victory over sin, I will share some of the ugly details that I would just as soon forget.

I must tell you this part of my life to demonstrate the power of Jesus Christ, who said in Luke 4:18-19,

> "*The Spirit of the Lord is on me, because he has anointed me to preach good news to the poor.*
>
> *He has sent me to proclaim freedom for the prisoners and recovery of sight for the blind, to release the oppressed, to proclaim the year of the Lord's favor.*"

The power of Jesus Christ is greater than ourselves, greater than all our sins. He releases the prisoners and sets them free.

After Dad passed away, my life started taking a downhill course, although I didn't realize it at the time.

One sunny day at our house in Walnut Creek on Old Pump Street, I was weeding one of Mom's beautiful flower beds. Polly, an older sister of some girls in our horse club, came by and stopped to chat. She was home from college, and it wasn't long until we were seeing more of each other on a casual friendship basis.

Polly began showing me a part of life that was new, a life in which I was very naive. I had grown up in a sheltered environment, but now curiosity drew me into exploring and experiencing new things. *What could be wrong with trying a few beers or a little whiskey or having a good time? I thought, I'll have my little fling in life and then I'll settle down and raise a family.*

When I joined the Mennonite Church, I had lost the base of friends I'd grown up with at Bethel Fellowship. Polly introduced me to a new circle, and I let myself be involved in the lifestyle and friendships of the party-goers. Little by little, I was caught up in a way of life that controlled me. I no longer controlled what I was doing.

Mom never said too much, but I know she knew I was drinking. One night, I threw up in my pickup on the way home. The next day she smelled what had happened. I told her I was sick, but she knew why I was sick. I remember one night at a party I sampled everyone's drink; I had everything from scotch, whiskey, beer—you name it, I drank it. My body could not handle that kind of abuse. I lay out on the barn floor that night, not able to move, puking my insides out, lying there in a stupor of drunkenness until morning.

On my way home the next day, I told myself I would not take another drink. But alcohol already had control of my life. During that time, I was teaching a junior high Sunday School class at church, and there were times I tried to teach a class of young people while I fought a hangover from Saturday night.

I was working for my Uncle Vernon as a tender on a mason crew. When Vernon ran low on cement on his cement board, he would holler at me, "Mud!" That meant he needed more cement. One day we were laying up a chimney at Lake Buckhorn, and the homeowner came by and asked Vernon if my name really was Mud. We had a good laugh over that one.

Vernon was an avid sportsman and hunter who taught me many things about nature and wildlife. On a spring day he would say, "It's too nice to work. Let's go fishing." So we'd take the day off and sit on the banks of the Killbuck, fishing for suckers.

Almost every spring there would always be a few days to hunt for morel mushrooms. To this day, when spring comes around and the leaves start coming out on the trees, I get spring fever and it's mushroom hunting time again. Finding a whole patch of the yellow sponge about four inches high feels like finding the mother lode of gold nuggets in the hills of California.

Vernon also taught me the art of deer hunting, where to look for trails, bedding areas, travel routes, scrapes, and buck rubs. I have killed my share of deer, but have never bagged the real big one.

I will never forget a hot muggy day on July 4, 1969. Vernon's crew was putting brick on a house in Berlin and the humidity was suffocating. We could hear rumblings of thunder in the distance all day long. We were still living on the farm in the Walnut Creek Bottom. That night after a tiring day at work, I fell asleep in our upstairs bedroom.

The next morning, I woke up to a world I had never seen before. There was water everywhere; all of the Walnut Creek Bottom was under water. Flooding, winds up to 100mph, tornadoes, and lightning caused 41 deaths and injured over

500 people. More than 10,000 homes were damaged and 104 small businesses were destroyed. A total rainfall of 10 to 14 inches in the span of about eight hours resulted in what was probably the most devastating flood in Ohio history. Along with Vernon's crew, I helped clean out flooded basements in the village of Killbuck, but the stench of mud and waste was almost unbearable.

My uncle Vernon taught me a lot about life and the outdoors. I thoroughly enjoyed those years I worked for him, but alcohol was beginning to control my life. I generally managed to stay sober during the week, but on the weekend it was usually a party or bar or maybe a trail ride where there was alcohol.

Sin is like a boa constrictor that wraps itself around its prey, trapping it, and soon squeezing the very life out of it. Sin was getting its grip on my life and I didn't even recognize it. People would talk to me about what I was doing, and I would just laugh at them. Church life was becoming less important and soon I stopped going altogether.

After Polly there was Rose; we met one night at a bar. We kept seeing each other at the bar on weekends. One night, I took her home and she told me the story of her life. She had a baby girl that was one year old. The father had denied all claim to the child and said it wasn't his. Rose's mom and dad were making it hard on her by denying her the love and affection she so desperately needed and craved. It was a sad case indeed, and my heart reached out to her.

I went home and thought about Rose's situation, and I came to the conclusion that I didn't want anything to do with her messed up life. The following weekend, sitting in front of her house in my 4x4 F150 Ford pickup, I told her that I wasn't going to be seeing her any more. It was like watching a balloon shrivel as the air escapes. Rose told me that if I left her, she was going to kill herself. In other words, if there was no one in this world that cared about her, she didn't want to go on in life. I really believed she might do it, and so I kept on seeing her.

I became very attached to Rose's little girl, Kim, and treated her just as if she had been my own daughter. I talked to Rose's mom and dad, and after that their relationship improved. In fact, Rose once told me, "I don't know what you did or said to them, but things have changed." She started getting her life back together, and by that time, I had fallen in love with her.

Our relationship lasted five years. The subject of marriage came up occasionally, but Rose said she would never feel accepted by my family. She eventually started seeing someone else, and I decided it would be the best for everyone if I cut all ties with Rose and Kim.

During my relationship with Rose, I started experimenting with marijuana, usually at parties where it would be passed around freely. I never did understand the big thrill of smoking this weed; I did it because other people were doing it. That was the thing to do at parties—sit around and pass a joint from one person to the next, something like Indians sitting in their wigwams passing a pipe. Maybe they discovered the marijuana weed long before the white man did.

One night after Rose and I had separated, I went out with a girl whose name I don't even remember. I do remember that we went to a bar in Canton, where she bought a pound of weed; then we went to someone's house and smoked pot and drank beer. Driving home on I-77 the next morning, I thought I was driving 90 mph, but I looked at the speedometer and was only doing 40.

One incident really scared me. I was high and driving home on old Route 39 between Sugarcreek and Walnut Creek. On the crest of a hill, I met a buddy of mine on a motorcycle. We were both left of center. It must have been the hand of God that prevented us from crashing into each other.

I began a new job, driving for a private trucking company hauling clay and coal. I liked driving truck better than carrying mud all day.

After I'd been at that job three years, my brother-in-law Ivan asked if I would like to work for the appliance company in Kidron, Ohio, where he was working. I worked there for sixteen years, delivering and installing water heaters, dishwashers, disposals, built-in ovens, cooktops, refrigerators, air conditioners. You name it, we installed it. Ivan was my mentor and Atlee Miller was my boss. I learned a lot of things from those two guys in the years I worked there. It was like getting a degree from a trade school with on-the-job training.

Soon after breaking up with Rose, I started dating April, a local Mennonite girl who worked as a secretary at the appliance store. Her dad wasn't very fond of me; he had heard stories about the wild life I was leading. I didn't really blame him; I probably wouldn't have wanted my daughter dating a guy like me, either.

April gave me a new outlook on life. I quit smoking and tried to stop drinking. I started jogging and getting my body in shape, and I'd even started going to church with her occasionally. We fell in love and were engaged to be married. I thought that finally my dreams of having a family were going to become reality.

Whoa. Not so fast. Love just didn't happen that way for me.

In the summer of 1978, April and her sister went on vacation. When they came home, I could tell that something was wrong. April wouldn't talk about it, but I sensed she really didn't want to see me anymore. Not wanting to press the issue, I decided to move on with my life.

After breaking up with April, I started looking back on my life, and the string of shattered and broken dreams was not a pretty picture. Ivan was married and had a career, and all my old buddies that I grew up with were married and had children and careers. Here I was, 29 years old, and feeling as though I just couldn't go on like this any longer.

I tried to change, but instead everything seemed to get worse. Some unseen force had a hold on my life that I could not break. I sought help from other people, but no one had an answer. I was spiraling in the grip of a depression I couldn't shake.

I could barely see anything in front of me. It was a dark August night, and no stars shone overhead. The blackness of the night mirrored the darkness and turmoil in my soul. Driving my pickup to an abandoned strip mine road not far from Walnut Creek, I was trying to find an answer to the struggle that was raging inside of me.

Ah, but there was Someone who knew where I was and what I was going through. Parking my truck, I got out and started walking in the darkness. All at once, I saw Jesus Christ himself.

In an instant, He showed me all the sins I had ever committed; they went flashing through my mind's eye. Then His words came like a sword, piercing my heart. *Why do you do these things? Of all the people that care about you, there is no one in the whole world that loves you as much as I do. You are hurting me.*

I have never seen such an expression of divine love as when I looked up into His face. His love radiated from His very being, and yet in that same face I also saw judgment. Overshadowed by His love, yes, but the judgment was there. I fell face down on the ground, weeping like a child, weeping with sorrow and remorse for my sins and the anguish I had caused my Savior Jesus Christ.

Time did stand still; there was no time. I have no clue

how long I was there. All I know is that when I got up, I was a free man. Jesus Christ had come and set me free from the demonic forces that had a grip on my life. He set me free from alcohol and drugs. I felt like a young heifer let out of her stall in the spring after a long hard winter, kicking up her heels, enjoying the freedom of the outdoors, as described in Malachi 4:2.

But for you who revere my name, the sun of righteousness will rise with healing in its wings. And you will go out and leap like calves released from the stall.

I could smell the flowers and trees and breathe in the fresh clean air. I felt I could fly like a bird that had been caged all her life. I could once again sing from my heart because there was joy unspeakable and full of glory. I had never felt so free in my whole life. John 8:36 says, "So if the Son sets you free, you will be free indeed."

For two weeks I experienced a high, but it wasn't from drugs or alcohol. No, it came from my heavenly Father who loved me so much that He sent his only Son Jesus Christ to set me free.

And my freedom also came because my earthly father

had prayed that his son would find the true love, joy, and peace that only Christ can give. I learned this from a note I found one day in my old conservative straight cut suit coat. I had not worn that suit since I had left our church at Bethel. Mom asked me to clean the old clothes out of her closet, and there in my coat pocket was a note from my dad, written years earlier, before he passed away. The note was my father's prayer for his son, a prayer that I would not just settle for church membership but that I would find genuine love and faith in Jesus Christ.

When my dad wrote that note, he probably could not imagine how his prayer would ever be answered, but I know that he must be rejoicing with the angels in heaven over his son that came home to his heavenly Father.

Thank you, Jesus. Thank you, Father. Thank you, Dad, for the love you showed to a son who had wandered off and found his way back home.

CHAPTER 3

Eve

Waylon Jennings sang a song about "looking for love in all the wrong places." That had been my life, but now my need and desire to find love and happiness in a marriage no longer controlled me. Now I had found the true love of my life, Jesus Christ. This love is greater than father or mother or wife could ever give, a love that satisfies the deepest need of our souls.

I now had an intense desire to know God's will for my life. Did God want me to serve Him in a foreign country or become a minister like my dad? I also thought, *Lord, I love to ski. I could be a witness for you on the ski slopes in Aspen as a ski patrol, or I could serve you somewhere in a warm climate with sandy beaches.*

As I was driving home one day from Cleveland with a load of appliances, an answer came just as clearly as if someone had spoken to me through the window of the truck. *You can serve me right where you are.*

I am not writing this book to make a name for myself or to praise anything I have done. My prayer to God has always been that if the story of my life and what He has done for me can help someone, can save one soul, then my life has been worth living. I give God all the honor and glory for what He has done in my life and what He continues to do today.

You may wonder what a vision is, what I really experienced that night. I know I was awake, but my mind was transported somewhere else by the power of Jesus Christ. Our lives are books; the pages are being written every day of our living. God created us and can access those books and show us what is written on those pages. There's probably truth to what some people relate when they say, "My life flashed before my eyes." Are these, perhaps, the books that are going to be opened at the judgment told about in Revelations 20:12, when the dead will be judged by what is written in the books?

One hot day in late August, as I jogged a three-mile route in our Walnut Creek neighborhood, I thought it would feel good to dive into a swimming pool to relax my muscles. I drove to the College of Wooster and took a swim in the indoor pool. After my swim, I stopped for a milkshake at McDonald's.

Temptations come in all shapes and forms, and temptation that day had both the shape and the form. In the car next to mine was a lady motioning for me to come to her car. This was a guy's dream come true—a gorgeous woman, cruising in a white Corvette convertible, inviting me to approach. I did, and that began my relationship with Bonnie.

Later, on a motorcycle trip through southern Ohio, Bonnie and I stopped at the Millersport Sweet Corn Festival. While we were riding one of the carnival rides, the gasoline engine powering the wheel was suddenly on fire. We were at the very top of the ride, almost thirty feet in the air, and flames shot up toward us. I was afraid the engine would explode and the whole structure would crash.

And here I was with a woman who was separated from her husband, doing things I should not have been doing. We did get off the ride safely, but I felt that God had sent me a warning.

When Bonnie invited me to move in with her, I realized that Satan was trying to get me right back into the life Jesus had brought me out of. No, I couldn't turn my back on

Christ and His love for me. I was going to follow Him. I ended the relationship with Bonnie.

Soon after that, I started dating Cindy, a Christian girl who was a senior in high school and a part-time secretary at the business where I worked. Cindy was bubbly and full of life, energetic and smart. She seemed more mature than I, even though I was twelve years older. I can still feel the butterflies that fluttered in my stomach that day as I sat in my mother's living room and called Cindy for the first time, asking her to go with me to a Cleveland Cavaliers game.

Cindy played on a girls' softball team, and she asked if I'd be willing to coach. This opened the door for me to connect with friends I didn't even realize I had. Cindy and I were often invited to go places and do things, and I especially remember the invitation to go water skiing. I loved skimming across the clear waters of a lake and jumping the wake.

We talked about getting married, but for perhaps the first time in my life I was just enjoying the thrill of living and I wasn't sure I wanted to be tied down to a committed relationship. So I told Cindy I wanted to break up for a while. I thought it would be a test; did God really want us to get married?

There I was, the dream of marriage waiting right in front of me. This was what I had always thought was my goal. But now I stepped back, debating whether this was what I really wanted.

Cindy later told me she spent most of the next week crying. We were only separated for that one week, because that's all it took for me to know that I could not be without her.

CHAPTER 4

God's Fabric

Cindy and I were married at Sonnenberg Mennonite Church on November 10, 1979. Three years later, we were expecting our first child. I made the announcement at work with a cake decorated with a picture of a pregnant woman. Chad was born on April 15, 1983; and as I looked down on that little child, my entire life changed. I was a father, and the awesome responsibility was suddenly very real to me.

A year later, in the spring of 1984, we began building a new house. My dream had always been to build a house that was not only our home but was also a place where strangers and friends alike would find a warm welcome. This new house would not be "our" house, but it would be everyone's house.

We dug the basement and footer. Then the spring rains started; and for an entire month, all I could do was watch a big hole fill up with water. After the rains finally stopped, I cleaned out the footer, got it poured, and worked on the house almost every evening until midnight. We finally moved into our new home in February of 1985.

Our daughter, Amber, was born the next year, on August 9, 1986. As our children grew, our family life was filled with work, school, ballgames, church, and all the activities surrounding raising a family. My most cherished times were the times our family spent at the dinner table, sharing our lives and daily activities. If you invest time with your children when they are young, it pays great dividends when they are grown.

But the course of our lives can be changed overnight. And that is what happened to our family. God moves in mysterious ways, His wonders to perform.

My grandmother, Sarah Troyer, was a seamstress who made Sunday suits for Amish men. My mother also made many intricately stitched quilts and embroidered pillows, which she sold in her little business called The Dresden Plate.

Just as my mother and grandmother created beautiful things out of fabric and thread or just as an artist takes a paint brush and creates a picture, so Jesus Christ's love comes into our hearts and creates something beautiful on the pages of our lives that will serve God's purpose and give Him the glory.

This is illustrated beautifully in the old poem by Myra Brooks Welch called "The Touch of the Master's Hand." The poem is about an old violin being sold at an auction. The auctioneer can only get a bid of three dollars, but an old man comes from the crowd, takes the violin, and plays a beautiful melody. Then the bidding begins again, and the violin is sold for three thousand dollars. The master's hand brought forth the beauty.

Both Chad and Amber excelled athletically, and they were very passionate about their chosen sports. Chad played baseball almost from the time he could walk, and he grew into an accomplished pitcher. As a freshman in high school, he played on the varsity team. His dream was to win a college scholarship and play college baseball as a pitcher.

Amber did well in softball and basketball, but volleyball was her great love. She was constantly knocking balls against our walls, working to improve her skills. She has always had that drive within her, the drive to excel at whatever she does. Even as a child playing with toys, she went all out until her batteries died. We called her the Energizer bunny.

Amber was playing basketball on her team's home floor, driving the ball down the court. Somehow she got tangled up with another player and hit the floor. No one thought the fall was serious, but in the days following, Amber suffered recurring mild headaches. She never wanted to bother other people with her problems and became very adept at covering up what was really going on. But I decided to take her to our family doctor, just to be on the safe side. An x-ray showed she had suffered a concussion.

We decided to see a neurologist in Canton. He prescribed pills for Amber, but first did an EKG, which is standard procedure to check for any effect the medication might have on the patient's heart. After reading the EKG, the doctor told us the results were abnormal and he sent us to another building to see a cardiologist.

Amber and I had gone to see the doctor about her head, and we ended up checking out her heart. Maybe that's a picture of some people's spiritual troubles; they think there's something wrong with the head, when it's actually a heart problem.

We trotted over to the heart doctor, where they put Amber on a cardiac ECHO machine that takes pictures of the heart. An hour later, we were in the doctor's office, waiting for the verdict.

The doctor told us that Amber had a condition called hypertrophic cardiomyopathy. I'd never heard this term, much less understood what it all meant. But as Amber and I walked back to our car, we looked at each other and we both knew that it meant our lives had just been drastically changed.

Research on the internet told us that this was an inherited heart condition, most often passed through the male gene pool. The muscles of the heart thicken and restrict the blood flow. The electrical impulses that flow through the heart are often also affected.

We began seeing a specialist at the Cleveland Clinic and learned that if Amber stayed on pills called beta blockers, she could lead a very normal life. There was one exception. She could not be involved in competitive sports, because that activity would put too much stress on her heart.

Everyone in the family was tested. Chad and I both had different varieties of the same condition. My condition was so mild that it barely showed in the test results. Chad's was more serious than mine, but not as advanced as Amber's.

It was very difficult for Chad to accept that he had to give up baseball. I took him to three different heart specialists. The third doctor told us stories of major league ballplayers who had the same condition but talked doctors into signing their health certificates. Those decisions had cost their lives. I looked over at Chad's face and could see in his eyes that he had given up his determination to play baseball and had accepted the fact that his life also had changed course.

The doctors did give Chad permission to play golf, and he loves to do that to this day. Amber had always loved music, so she threw her heart and energy into the music program at school.

I've often wondered how the lives of our children would be different today if they had pursued the courses they had been on. Instead, our children have found a passion to serve and follow Jesus Christ. For Cindy and me, that is worth far more than any sports trophy sitting in some obscure room collecting dust.

There have been many times I have wept, wishing I could give new hearts to our children. But God really does know what is best for us as He weaves the fabric of our lives.

CHAPTER 5

Arrested

Life was pretty good. At least, that's the way it looked from the outside.

My closet-organizing business was going well and Cindy had a good job. We had friends and family all around us, and Chad and Amber were excelling at school.

But without realizing what was happening, I had been letting the activities of daily life take priority and putting God in a back room somewhere. As a result, I started to struggle in my spiritual walk with Christ.

Friday, December 6, 2002, was just like any other Friday. I was working on closets in a new house about five miles from my home. About 11:30, my phone rang. It was Cindy, calling to tell me to leave immediately and meet her at Amber's school. Something had happened to our daughter.

I wasn't too worried about this; Amber had occasional weak spells and pain in her heart. But as I drove to the school, Cindy called again to say the ambulance had just passed her on the road and we needed to go to a local hospital.

There we were met by Terry Shue, a local Mennonite pastor, and also Richard Ross, a friend and chaplain at the hospital. Rita, Amber's mentor, was also there to meet us. Things didn't look good. Amber had suffered cardiac arrest. We found her lying on a table in the emergency room, unconscious. Her local heart specialist had been in the hospital when Amber was brought in, and he had given her a shot to paralyze her muscles, but they wanted to get her to a larger hospital immediately.

Life Flight was called to transport her to Aultman Hospital in Canton. We decided that Cindy would ride to the Canton hospital with Rita, and I would go home and get out of my work clothes. On the way home, I stopped at the school to piece together what had happened that morning.

A group of student singers had walked a short distance downtown to sing for a lady on her birthday. As they returned to school, Amber had collapsed in the school driveway.

God's hand had prepared for this emergency. Knowing Amber's condition, someone had donated an external defibrillator to the school, so that was now available immediately. A nurse who worked in the cardiac unit at the hospital was driving by when Amber collapsed, and she felt compelled to stop and help. The local EMTs had just returned from another run and were all in town.

As nearly as I could calculate, it was about seven to ten minutes from the time Amber's heart stopped until it was shocked and restarted. That was long enough for some brain damage to occur.

The first person I met as I walked into the cardio intensive care unit was a doctor who told me that the most important thing Amber needed was prayer. I knew we were in good hands; many people were praying for us.

During the night, Cindy fell asleep on a chair in the lobby and I sat beside Amber in her room. At two in the morning, Amber opened her eyes for the first time since she had collapsed. It was all I could do to keep my emotions in check and give her a smile. Amber was back with us.

She had short-term memory loss, and couldn't remember things from one minute to the next. Over the next week, her memory started coming back. To this day, though, there is one week of her life that is completely blank. Amber does not recall anything from one Thanksgiving weekend when we were with all of Cindy's family at Atwood Lodge. That week has never returned to her.

During her hospital stay, Amber had surgery to install an implanted defibrillator and pacemaker. She'll probably wear these the rest of her life.

I am telling you Amber's story because it profoundly changed the course of my life. It has so changed my life that I am fairly certain I would not even be writing this book had we not gone through this experience.

As life returned to normal, I started to see more vividly how the hand of God had been in all of these events. What was the meaning, the purpose of what had happened? What was God trying to tell us? According to our doctor in Cleveland, this episode should never have happened. I was like Daniel, wanting to know God's plan and purpose.

I was pondering all these questions when God spoke to me so clearly that I knew I could do nothing other than obey what He was telling me.

You might ask how I can know when God speaks to

me. I might ask you, how do you know you are stealing from someone? Is someone there, telling you you're doing something wrong? Yes, it's called your conscience, an inner voice speaking to you. The Bible says, Seek and ye shall find; knock and it will be opened unto you. In my experience, when we seek God with a sincere heart we will usually hear from Him. And often, God speaks to us in a way we never expected.

The message I received was straight from God's word: "Can you not stay awake with me for one hour?"

Yes, that was it. God was asking me to give Him one hour of my time every day, spent in prayer and reading His word.

I would get up about 4:30 in the morning, go into our office, check the time, then drop to my knees, talking to God. Usually I spent 45 minutes in prayer and 15 minutes reading God's word. For three months, I was duty-bound and compelled to obedience in keeping my end of the bargain.

I don't remember everything I prayed about, but I kept a mental prayer list. After a time, I noticed something had changed. God was changing my heart, my attitudes, and my desires. And the more my heart changed, the more of Himself God revealed to me. I was talking to a God who was real and living inside me. The word of God came alive and spoke to my heart. Its meaning became real. His words "are Spirit and they are life" (John 6:63).

This is the communion Adam and Eve had with God before they sinned, and it was like I, too, was walking in a garden of love, joy, and peace. I no longer looked at the clock, checking the time.

God laid things on my heart to pray for at all hours of the day and night. He was showing me that He wants to have a relationship with me, my family, my church family, my friends, my enemies. In fact, God is inviting people all over the world to have a living, breathing, life-giving relationship with him through his Son, Jesus Christ.

Just as in Jesus' time, many people today are looking for miracles or experiences. We want to see a person get out of a wheelchair and walk; we want to see a blind person able to see. We want to hear some fantastic revelation on end time prophetic events. We want to be caught in an emotional experience or spiritual high. But like skydiving from a plane or bungee jumping off a bridge or riding an extreme roller coaster, the experience does give you an adrenaline rush and makes you feel like you can conquer anything, but it will not satisfy the inner longings of your soul. After the rush is over, there is still the emptiness inside. We are left empty and disappointed because instead of seeking Jesus in our hearts we are seeking to satisfy an emotional craving that makes us feel good for a short time.

Jesus said in Matthew 12:39, "A wicked and adulterous generation asks for a miraculous sign! But none will be given it except the sign of the prophet Jonah." The sign Jesus was talking about was His resurrection.

Zaccheus was a short man (Luke 19), but he desired to see Jesus. So he went ahead of the crowd and climbed a sycamore tree. Little did he know that he was about to receive the greatest miracle of all, the miracle of salvation. Because of his heart's desire to see Jesus, he received the desire of his heart. In these last days that we are living in, are we looking for signs and wonders or are we looking for Jesus?

The Samaritan woman came to the well out of her need for water. The normal time for women to draw water was in the evening when women would go to the well with each other (Gen. 24:11). But she came at noon, by herself. She was there at this time, by herself, because of her greater need to satisfy the thirst in her soul. You see, she was trying to satisfy her inner longing for love through relationships with men. This made her an outcast among the other women in the village.

When she met Jesus at the well and he told her everything that was in her heart, she commented that there was only one man who could explain everything and that he was called Messiah. Jesus declared, "I who speak to you am he." Here she had met the Messiah, who could see right into her heart and show her what she really needed. She went into the village and proclaimed the good news. It says that many Samaritans from that town believed because of the woman's testimony. "He told me everything I ever did."

Are you looking for miracles or are you looking for Jesus, who can give you the miracle you really need?

After my wonderful experience of meeting Jesus, after the emotional high was wearing off, I decided to go back to the same place to see if maybe I could capture some of the same experience; maybe it was still in this place. I didn't fully comprehend that the experience was in Jesus and not in a place.

I drove my truck back to the strip mines, to the same place, at about the same time of night. I got out. It was so dark, I could hardly see. Suddenly, I heard the CB antenna on the top of my truck whipping back and forth, as though someone had pulled it down and let it fly. I sensed the presence of something evil and felt someone warning me to get out of there. I got in my truck and drove off as quickly as possible.

It taught me a valuable lesson to not look back but forward, looking unto Jesus, the author and the finisher of our faith. Don't look to men who claim to have great powers, but put your faith and trust in Jesus Christ, who has been given all dominion, authority, and power (1 Cor. 15:24-28).

You say you believe in God and believe that He created all things. Jesus said, "If you believe in God, believe also in me." You cannot separate the two. He said, "I and the Father are one, and you cannot come to the Father except through me." *To know the love of the Father, we have to know the Son He loves.*

CHAPTER 6

Love

An ancient poem composed in 1096 by a Jewish songwriter, Rabbi Mayer, in Worms, Germany, speaks of a miracle which some think is the giving of the Ten Commandments. This poem is still read on the first day of the Feast of Shavuot (Fall Harvest, Festival of Weeks, begun seven weeks after Passover) before the reading of the Ten Commandments.

The poem describes God's eternal love for His people. One section reads:

> *Were the sky of parchment made,*
> *A quill each reed, each twig and blade.*

Could we with ink the oceans fill,
Were every man a scribe of skill,
The marvelous story of God's great glory
Would still remain untold;
For He, most high, the earth and sky
Created alone of old.

You may recognize these words, very like the third stanza of one of the greatest songs ever written. This old poem moved Fredrick M. Lehman to write the song we know as "The Love of God."

The whole creation shouts of God's love. The sun comes up every morning because God loves us. In the evening, we can sit and watch God's creation being put to bed under magnificent sunsets. In winter, the snow comes and covers the earth with a blanket of white, bringing a beauty that only God can create. In spring, the streams and rivers, trees and flowers and plants burst forth with new life. David spoke of this awe-inspiring creation of God in Psalm 19:1-6.

The heavens declare the glory of God; the skies proclaim the work of his hands.

Day after day they pour forth speech; night after night they display knowledge.

There is no speech or language where their voice is not heard.

Their voice goes out into all the earth, their words to the ends of the world. In the heavens he has pitched a tent for the sun,

which is like a bridegroom coming forth from his pavilion, like a champion rejoicing to run his course.

It rises at one end of the heavens and makes its circuit to the other; nothing is hidden from its heat.

All of creation is praising its Creator, its Maker. The birds sing, the oceans roar, the trees bow in the wind and give off a song as the wind passes through their branches. All things in nature are doing what God created them to do. All except man, who goes his own way because of sin.

Looking back on my life, I realize how very close I walked to the precipice of hell. Nothing I did made me deserving to be rescued by Jesus. Still to this day, I cannot explain or fathom the depths of God's love and grace. I can only try to describe it in a song the Lord inspired in me.

I can never repay you for the debt I owe
For what you did on the cross in saving my soul.

Through all of eternity, I'll give you praise
For your gift of love and amazing grace.

You see God would not have had to do anything to rescue us from our sins, but he did because He loves us with a love so deep, so strong, that it goes beyond any human love. It is divine love, a love that comes from only one source, God Himself.

Marilyn Laszlo, a highly educated Indiana farm girl, felt the call of God on her life to bring the gospel of Jesus Christ to native people in the jungles of Papua New Guinea. Dedicating twenty-four years of her life to the Sepik Iwam people, who had a history of head-hunting, sorcery, and deep hostility toward outsiders, she worked with Wycliffe Bible Translators to translate the New Testament and parts of the Old into the native language. Today, these people are missionaries themselves, bringing the message of Jesus to other tribes.

This missionary spoke at our church one Sunday morning, and the joy on her face spoke of the love, faith, and trust in her Savior Jesus Christ that brought her through the many trials she faced. People have asked her if she wasn't afraid. Her answer has stayed with me ever since: The safest place to be is in the center of God's will.

With tears of joy, I watched a video of these native men, in modern civilization for the first time in their lives, now standing on the stage of a Billy Graham crusade and quoting a verse from 1 John 4:7, "For love comes from God." You could tell that they had found the greatest treasure that anyone can ever find, the love of God.

For God so loved the world he gave his only begotten Son, that whosoever believeth in him should not perish but have everlasting life (John 3:16).

This is how God showed his love among us: He sent his one and only Son into the world that we might live through him. This is love: not that we loved God, but that he loved us and sent his Son as an atoning sacrifice for our sins (1 John 4:9-10).

We cannot earn this divine Love, we have to receive it from the only source, from God through Jesus Christ, as we surrender our lives to him. In 2 Corinthians 2:14, Paul describes a life that knows God as a fragrance that spreads everywhere. Mary demonstrated it in John 12:3, when she poured expensive perfume on Jesus' feet and wiped it with her hair; the fragrance filled the whole house. Peter and John lived it in Acts 4:13, when the rulers took note that these men had been with Jesus. To some, this fragrance is the smell of death; to others, the fragrance of life (2 Cor. 2:16).

Serving Jesus Christ is not a "have to". No, it is a "want to", because of His love in our hearts. "We love because he first loved us" (1 John 4:19). "Love comes from God" (1 John 4:7). You could spend your whole life on the mission fields spreading the gospel or feeding the poor, but 1 Corinthians 13 says that if you don't do it out of love, it is all for naught.

You see, a relationship with Jesus Christ is all about love. It is a lot like our relationships with our spouses, if we truly love each other. We don't do things for our spouses and children because it's required or because we fear getting into trouble. Instead, we choose to do things for our family because we love them.

We were making preparations for our daughter Amber's wedding. About two weeks before the wedding, she decided that she wanted me to build a cloth canopy over the whole gymnasium where the reception would be held.

I was going through a lot of stress at that time, and I informed her that this was an unnecessary headache that I didn't need and a floor and food tables and maybe a few decorations were all that were required. I told her that weddings were about the three Fs—Fun, Food, Fellowship.

But for girls, that wedding day is the most special day of their lives. Anyhow, daughters and moms usually always win out at wedding planning, and we men have to go with the plan and just bear it.

So we strung up wire and canopy overhead and were just ready to put up the lights when one end of the cable holding the canopy came loose. I could just imagine sitting at the reception with the whole thing coming down, covering everyone with yards of cloth.

At this point, I was ready to give up and throw in the towel, but I got a word of encouragement from our pastor who had just stopped by.

"Rob," he told me, "You can do it. It will look beautiful. We do it *because we love them.*"

That phrase gave me the motivation I needed. I got stronger cable and rings (which I should have done in the first place), and with the help of friends got the canopy up—with lights and the whole enchilada.

Needless to say, there were many oohs and ahs at the magic created by canopy and lights that night. I was in awe of the whole thing myself. The best part was still the Fun, Food, and Fellowship, but I had helped to create a wonderful wedding day memory for my daughter. I did it because I loved her.

Serving Christ is not forced performance but grows out of love. When we serve God to earn rewards or just because we hope to get to heaven, we are missing the whole point of who God really is. God is love. He created the universe and everything in it, and He created man in His own image—all because of love.

God wants to have a relationship with us, not because He demands it, but because He loves us.

CHAPTER 7

The Heart

But, you say, if God is a God of love, if He loves us so much, why do so many bad things happen in the world? Why is there misery and suffering? Why was my son killed in a car accident? Why was my daughter raped and murdered? How can a God of love allow things like this to happen? What about God's judgment and his wrath upon mankind and what about hell?

Maybe you won't believe it when I tell you that it is all because "God is love" (1 John 4:16). The whole essence of His being is love. You see, God created man to have a relationship with him, and He created man not to be robots but with the capacity to choose to follow God. We cannot argue with God about why He made us this way, because He is God and He can do whatever He wants. Isaiah 45:9 says, "Woe to him who quarrels with his maker. Does the clay say to the potter, 'What are you making'?"

But when we choose to follow our own plans instead of God's, we bring judgment upon ourselves. In the very beginning when God created man He also created judgment. His judgment was put in place in Genesis 2:16-17 when "the LORD God commanded the man, 'You are free to eat from any tree in the garden; but you must not eat from the tree of the knowledge of good and evil, for when you eat of it you will surely die.'"

Amber and I were flying to Washington, D.C., the heart of our nation, where laws are made that affect our lives. I'd always wanted to visit this city, but had never been there, perhaps because Cindy has so little interest in politics.

Through a recommendation from Dr. Terry Gordon, a cardiologist with The Heart Group in Akron, Ohio, Amber joined 41 other survivors of sudden cardiac arrest who were invited to the first SCA Survivor Summit in Washington, D.C. Sponsored by the National Center for Early Defibrillation, this summit intended to increase awareness of SCA (sudden cardiac arrest) and to promote automated external defibrillators (AEDs). The number of attendees, 42, is the approximate number of incidents of SCA every hour here in the United States. The frequency of SCA is higher than breast cancer, AIDS, car accidents, and house fires combined. Of people who experience sudden cardiac arrest, 93 percent do not survive.

Amber and I flew into Washington's Dulles airport on October 2, 2003. We stayed at the Hyatt Regency, where the conference was held. The highlight of our trip was not to see the sights of Washington, but to hear the stories of survivors. All 42 survivors shared what had happened to them and how they had survived. People from all walks of life, ages 12 to 74, from more than twenty states, told their stories. It was a very emotional time, to say the least.

Why is there pain and suffering in this world?

On September 11, 2001, I came home at 9:30 in the morning, turned on the television, and watched with the rest of the world as the World Trade Center collapsed, killing almost three thousand people. Just recently, we watched in horror and awe as the saga of earthquake and tsunami unfolded in Japan.

Closer to home, I recently walked into Boyd & Wurthmann Restaurant and met a woman about my age that I haven't seen for almost thirty years. She shared with me the pain she was going through after the loss of her mother and some of her closest friends. Her overwhelming grief was heart-wrenching. Why must we endure such suffering?

I was reading the book of Job recently and found a new perspective on Job's story. This story is really about the epic struggle between good and evil.

God is the author of good. Jesus said, "No one is good—except God alone" (Mark 10:18). Satan is the author of evil; he may even use the goodness in man to achieve his evil purposes.

God, though, uses Satan's plans for evil to bring about His good. Romans 8:28 tells us that God works for the good of those who love Him. We see the ultimate example of this in the crucifixion of Christ. Satan thought he had destroyed his greatest adversary, when in fact he had just sealed his own fate.

Here's my modern version of Job's story, set in our own times.

Our characters are all very successful, college-educated businessmen who had grown up together and shared their hopes and dreams. They had families, built new homes, and grew 401K plans on track for early retirement. Growing up in Christian homes, they had all become Sunday School teachers and church elders.

Now they hear about their friend Job's troubles, and decide to go visit him. Surely there must be a reason that Job was having all this misfortune; surely there must be something wrong in his life that he was not telling them. The three visitors know a lot about God, but don't really have personal relationships with Him. They describe God and His ways in elegant words.

So we see here an arrogance in Christian attitude. Do we put ourselves a little above everyone else? But God says His ways are far beyond our understanding.

For who has known the mind of the LORD that he may instruct him? (1 Cor. 2:16)

"For my thoughts are not your thoughts, neither are your ways my ways," declares the LORD (Isa. 55:8).

In the end, God speaks to Job and says, "How can any of you know what I'm up to? Why don't you confront me about this, instead of trying to come up with your own answers? You guys don't know what you're talking about."

Job was humbled and said, "I spoke of things I did not understand." And the Lord told Job's three friends they'd better have Job pray for them, because "I will accept his prayers, but not yours."

God is not the instigator of suffering, but He allows it to happen for our own good. Suffering and trials break down the hard and crusty soil of our hearts. It's difficult to plant seed in the middle of the summer when the ground is hard; and even though rains come, the water cannot penetrate the soil deeply. Instead, the farmer plants his crops in the spring, when the soil is soft and pliable.

This is the kind of heart soil that God wants. A heart of humility recognizes that it does not have all the answers. God desires a relationship and our honesty with Him more than He wants our good works. Psalm 51:17 says, "The sacrifices of God are a broken spirit; a broken and contrite heart, O God, you will not despise."

When we no longer *tell* God to bless us in the plans *we* have made, but instead come to Him with broken hearts that recognize our need of Him, then God can shape and mold us into what He wants us to be. And we can't fool

Him. "Man looks at the outward appearance, but the LORD looks at the heart" (1 Sam. 16:7).

I thank God for the suffering and pain I've gone through. The love He has for me and the intimate relationship we share far outweigh all of my life's struggles. **I have found a wealth that cannot be measured on an earthly scale; it's stored in the treasure vault of heaven, in the heart of God.**

CHAPTER 8

The Author

Is God writing on the pages of our hearts with His ink of love, or are we trying to write our own stories with the ink of selfish ambition? These two different stories have been written in the pages of history from the beginning of time. From the days of Adam and Eve, Cain and Abel, Jacob and Esau to you and me today, the stories will be played out in the hearts of people until the end of time. The two thieves hanging on crosses beside Jesus represent these two types of individuals. One realized his sentence was what he deserved; the other tried to use Jesus to escape his deserved punishment.

We can never know the breadth, the depth, the height of God's love, but when His love comes and lives in our hearts, it starts to melt away all the sin and dirty things in our lives. Malachi 3:2-3 says he will be like a refiner's fire or a launderer's soap. He will sit as a refiner and purifier of silver.

For some people, it may take a little more scrubbing and refining than for others, depending on how stubborn we are in letting go of things in our lives. A story read to us third graders by our teacher, Edith Troyer, has stayed with me through the years. It was called "The North Wind and the Sun."

The north wind and the sun argued about which of them was the stronger. To settle their argument, they decided to see which one had the power to make a traveler take off his coat.

The north wind started the contest, sending a strong blast of cold air to blow the coat off the man's back. Instead of taking off his coat, the man wrapped it around his body even tighter.

The sun laughed at his opponent's failure. Then he showed his power. He melted the heavy clouds from the sky and warmed the head of the traveler. The man in his heavy coat started to suffer from the heat. At last, unable to bear the heat any longer, the man removed his coat and sat down in the shade of a tree.

Let's say the coat represents sins in our lives. The point is, we cannot get rid of sin ourselves. If we try to get rid of our sin on our own, we are just reforming ourselves into a different version of our old selves. The only way to be transformed is through power of Jesus Christ, represented by the sun. He is the only one who has the power to remove sin in our lives.

If we confess our sins, he is faithful and just and will forgive us our sins and purify us from all unrighteousness (1 John 1:9).

So the warmth of Christ's love as we have fellowship with Him makes us want to confess our sins and let Him cleanse us and purify, shape, and mold us. He transforms us into the image of Christ himself. This is called the sanctification process, cleansing us from our sins through His blood.

This transformation process takes place through the power of the Holy Spirit. John 6:63 says, "The Spirit gives life; the flesh counts for nothing. The words I have spoken to you are spirit and they are life."

When this process takes place in our lives, then we can say with Paul in Romans 8:1-2, "Therefore, there is now no condemnation for those who are in Christ Jesus, because through Christ Jesus the law of the Spirit of life set me free from the law of sin and death."

Paul says in Hebrews 12:2 that Jesus Christ is "the author and perfecter of our faith." The King James translation uses the words "the author and finisher." It is no longer I who am trying to live a good life, but it is the Spirit of Life in Christ at work in me, that lets me live in freedom from sin.

The Spirit of Christ inside me is more real than anything I can see, touch, smell, or hear. Jesus said, "I have come that you might have life and have it more abundantly." He said, "I am the bread of life, and I am the way, the truth, the life."

Do we have to wait until Jesus returns to have this life? No. We can have the life of Christ living in our hearts today.

I have an intense desire for people to know this living, breathing, life-giving relationship with Jesus Christ. Why do people just want to talk about their jobs, their families, the weather? Of course, there is absolutely nothing wrong with sharing your life experiences; the only thing is, these things are superficial and temporary; they don't last. You buy a new car, but as soon as you drive it off the lot, its value drops. Houses and possessions are lost through hurricanes, tornadoes, fire, and floods. Jobs come and go, children grow up and get married, we get older and we die. So is this life, or is there something more than just existing and dying? Is that all life is, or is this life just a temporary stepping stone to something far greater?

I see a lot of empty, shallow, ritualistic worship, a form of godliness, but no power. Many people do good things, but it comes out of duty or promotion of a cause rather than from a heart of genuine love for Christ. "If I give all I possess to the poor and surrender my body to flames, but have not love, I gain nothing" (1 Cor. 13:3).

How can I change people's hearts? How can I get people motivated and passionate to serve and follow Jesus Christ? How can I give people this life in Christ?

The truth is, I can't give this life to you. We can build big fancy cathedrals and churches; we can have the best worship teams that money can buy and all the nurturing programs, books, Bible studies, the best speakers, teachers and preachers. But there is only one way you can have this life within you, and that is by God putting his Spirit within you through His Son, Jesus Christ.

Jesus said, "Unless the Father draws you, you cannot come to me." I am convinced that unless the Spirit of God moves and touches the heart of people, change doesn't really take place. The reality is, we can't even save ourselves. If we could save ourselves, then God would not get the glory and man would become God himself. The Bible says that our own righteousness is as filthy rags. Man trying to control his own destiny is like a sailor trying to navigate the ocean without a sail, rudder, or compass. Man can reform someone, but Jesus Christ is the only One that can transform the heart. Jesus Christ is the only one that can take away our desire to sin.

So how can we be saved and have the life of Christ within us?

First, we have to realize that we are lost without hope, without God. No one can be saved if he does not realize that he is lost.

Let's say two buddies, Joe and Eli, are hiking. They get off on the wrong trail. Joe says, "I think we're going the wrong way. I'm going to turn around and go back and ask for help."

Eli says, "I know we're on the right trail. I'm going to keep on going."

Joe goes back and finds help, and they send out a search party to find Eli. Someone finds Eli and says, "I've come to help you find your way out."

Eli says, "I don't need help. I'm on the right trail." And he keeps on going.

Jesus said, "I have come to seek and to save that which was lost" (Luke 19:10). So who is lost? All of us, for all have sinned and fallen short of the glory of God. There is none righteous, not one of us. Our righteousness comes only from the Author of righteousness.

How do I get the righteousness of Jesus Christ? There

is only one way that this can happen, and that is by dying on the cross with Christ. Dying to the selfish me. Dying to what I want. Then and only then can I be resurrected to a new life in Christ.

I have been crucified with Christ and I no longer live, but Christ lives in me. The life I live in the body, I live by faith in the Son of God, who loved me and gave himself for me (Gal 2:20).

On Sunday morning, December 12, 2004, in my office on my knees, I received a message from God so real, so powerful, that my whole body was weak. The message was, *The midnight cry is going forth; the awaking is coming.*

I immediately knew this referred to the story of the ten virgins in Matthew 25:6. This means that before Christ returns, God is going to move in a very real way to give people one last opportunity to repent and turn to Jesus Christ.

"For the message of the cross is foolishness to those who are perishing, but to us who are being saved it is the power of God" (1 Cor. 1:18). Noah worked at building the ark for 120 years, and people laughed and said there was no flood coming.

But when God shut the door to the ark, it was too late for the scoffers to be saved from the flood. So it will be when God's Spirit is no longer drawing people to Christ. The door of those hearts will be shut, and it will be too late to be saved.

CHAPTER 9

Faith

My dad was not perfect, and I am not perfect; but I can come into the presence of God through the One who is perfect. That One is Jesus Christ, the Son of God, the perfect sacrifice and atonement for our sins.

We can earn no merits or rewards that are good enough to allow us to stand in the presence of the holy and almighty God. The only access we have to God the Father is through Jesus Christ, who is our high priest. He is the intermediary between the believer and God.

*Therefore since we have a great high priest who
has gone through the heavens, Jesus the Son of God,
let us hold firmly to the faith we profess (Heb. 4:14).*

We must realize our utter hopelessness as sinners, come
into the presence of God through Jesus Christ, and say,
"Make me as one of your hired servants."

*You do not delight in sacrifice, or I would bring
it; you do not take pleasure in burnt offerings.*
*The sacrifices of God are a broken spirit; a
broken and contrite heart, O God, you will not
despise (Ps. 51:16-17).*

*If we claim to be without sin, we deceive
ourselves and the truth is not in us.*
*If we confess our sins, he is faithful and just
and will forgive us our sins and purify us from all
unrighteousness (1 John 1:8-9)*

Every human being that has ever lived has messed up
somewhere in his life. There has never been a perfect system
of government or a perfect religion. Only one person who was
born of a woman and walked this earth has lived a perfect life.

That person is Jesus Christ, the Son of God. "He committed no sin, and no deceit was in his mouth" (1 Pet. 2:22).

If we have faith and trust in Him, Jesus Christ will enable us also to live a life of victory over sin.

> ...for everyone born of God overcomes the world. This is the victory that has overcome the world, even our faith.
>
> Who is it that overcomes the world? Only he who believes that Jesus is the Son of God (1 John 5:4-5).

Many Christian people live their lives in defeat because they try to overcome sin by their own power. When Christ died on the cross, He took our sins to the cross with Him. His sacrifice was for all our sins, and He does not have to die on the cross every time we sin.

> Unlike the other high priests, he does not need to offer sacrifices day after day, first for his own sins, and then for the sins of the people. He sacrificed for their sins once for all when he offered himself (Heb. 7:27).

So why do people who believe Christ saved them from

their sins keep struggling with sin throughout their lives? We struggle if we lack faith; or, to say it for what it is, we struggle because of unbelief.

We don't really trust Christ if we can't surrender everything to Him. Unbelief is when we subconsciously tell Christ that He can have certain parts of our lives, but other parts we want to keep for ourselves.

When they are little, most kids have a security blanket or stuffed animal that they must have with them when they go to bed. We have a photograph of our daughter at three, standing by the clothesline. Her blanket had been washed and was hanging there to dry. Amber has one thumb in her mouth, and the other hand is clutching a corner of her blanket. Many Christians hang on to things in their lives just as tightly, because hanging on gives them a sense of security and control.

The very thing that you are unwilling to relinquish is the thing Satan can use to attack you. If you are unwilling to let go, you do not have on the whole armor of God. It may be your business, your money, your home, your family, or your children. Maybe you can't let go of sports, computer games, or pornography. Whatever you have not surrendered to the authority of Jesus Christ is the thing that is keeping you from living in freedom and victory.

Jesus said in Matthew 10:37-39 that those who cannot let go are not worthy of Him.

"Anyone who loves his father or mother more than me is not worthy of me; anyone who loves his son or daughter more than me is not worthy of me; and anyone who does not take his cross and follow me is not worthy of me.

Whoever finds his life will lose it, and whosever loses his life for my sake will find it."

The cross Jesus is talking about here is whatever Christ is calling you to do. The cross symbolizes surrender and sacrificing your life for the sake of Christ and His purpose. Is he calling you to stay at home and teach your children? Or maybe He wants you to be a missionary in a foreign country. Perhaps He wants you to be a minister. Or He might be asking you simply to share His message and love in your daily life. But He is asking you to do something.

"Take my yoke upon you and learn from me for I am gentle and humble in heart, and you will find rest for your souls.

For my yoke is easy and my burden is light" (Matt. 11:29-30).

The yoke symbolizes your connection with Christ in the calling He has for your life. In Jesus' time, the yoke was used to pair two oxen together, and the oxen were then attached to a wagon or plow. At home on the farm, when we wanted to train a young draft horse to work the fields, we would hitch him to an older, more mature horse. The younger horse could learn from the older one.

Jesus was trying to teach us that when we take up our cross and follow Him, we are yoked together with Him in living His will and purpose for our lives. Being yoked with Him will see us through suffering, hardship, pain, grief, or anything else we face. He is right there with us.

Through our faith in Christ, we can overcome any obstacle or stumbling block that we face in life. When Christ died on the cross, He didn't just take our sins with Him, but He defeated the powers that cause *tempt* us to sin. *Entices*

> In Christ all the fullness of the Deity lives in
> bodily form,
>   and you have been given fullness in Christ,
> who is the head over every power and authority
> (Col. 2:9-10).

And having disarmed the powers and authorities, he made a public spectacle of them, triumphing over them by the cross (Col. 2:15).

So is it possible to live a victorious life in Christ? Absolutely, by realizing we can't do it on our own and by putting our faith in Christ, who has destroyed the power of sin, death, and hell. Then the power of Christ through the Holy Spirit enables us to live a life that is free from sin and is a witness for Him.

But as many as received him, to them gave he power to become the sons of God even to them that believe on his name (John 1:12).

"My righteous one will live by faith. And if he shrinks back, I will not be pleased with him" (Heb. 10:38).

Without faith, it is impossible to please God (Heb 11:6).

Faith is at work when we can say, "See what God is doing." If, instead, we are saying, "See what I am doing," we are exalting ourselves; this is not of faith. Faith in Christ doesn't have to brag or boast, but it is motivated by the love of Christ within us to do His will instead of our own will.

Faith in Christ is like stepping on an airplane to fly to a destination. You are putting your faith in the pilot to get you there safely. Jesus Christ has gone the way before us, and by putting our faith in Him, He will lead us to our destination, so that where He is, there we may be also (John 14:3).

Faith in Christ is holding on to the promises He has given us. I will never leave you nor forsake you. Cast all your cares on me, for I care for you. I will guide you into all truth. And many more.

Faith in Christ is not a one-time deal where you accept Christ and now you're going to heaven. Faith in Christ becomes your life. "For you died, and your life is now hidden with Christ in God. When Christ, who *is* your life, appears, then you also will appear with him in glory" (Col 3:3-4).

When we yield our lives completely to Jesus Christ, we are no longer bound to things in the earthly realm but are connected by Jesus Christ to things in the heavenly realm. *We will not be limited to what man can accomplish; but we will begin to see the unlimited possibilities for God to accomplish His purpose in our lives.*

Our world is in a sad mess because people are not

connected to God, the power source. Jesus taught us to pray saying, "Thine is the kingdom, Thine is the power, Thine is the glory." *The greatest display of power God has demonstrated to mankind is the power demonstrated in the resurrection and forgiveness of our sins.*

If you carry a watch with you but don't put a battery in your watch, you can say, "I have a watch," but it won't serve any purpose. You might say you know God, but unless you are truly connected to Him, there will be no power in your life.

CHAPTER 10

Prayer

Recently, I stood in the lunch line at a two-day Bible conference and started a casual conversation with the tall man in front of me. I had never met him before, but after I had my food and found a seat, he walked over to my table and asked if he could sit with me. During our time together, he told me he was in the process of writing a book, but he did not know if it would ever be published.

I asked him what his book was about, and discovered the man was writing about his father, who had walked out on his wife and children. Ever since he was a little boy, this man had been fatherless and had never known a father's love. I was in the process of writing my book about the love of two fathers in my life.

It was no coincidence that we met that day.

You see, not too long ago, I began to ask God to let me be a witness for Him, not some time in the future, but today, now, here. When we pray a prayer like this in honesty, we had better be prepared to meet and talk with people in the most unexpected places. Again and again, I've been amazed at the hand of God bringing two people together. Many times, I've come home and told Cindy, "You won't believe who I talked with today."

God not only answered that prayer of my heart, He did so with a sense of humor. Jesus said, "But thou, when thou prayest, enter into thy closet" (Matthew 6:6 KJV). And God called me --- someone in the closet business --- to a ministry of prayer.

One Sunday morning, instead of going immediately to class, I went to the prayer room to have a conversation with God. Afterward, I noticed a man sitting alone in the coffee shop, and I sensed that sitting and conversing with him was more important than going to Sunday School class.

He told me of his conversation with God when he had faced a major surgery and knew there was a high probability he would not survive the procedure. He told God he was ready to go, if that was God's will for him, but that his desire was to spend a little more time with his family.

After his talk with God, a peace, calm, and joy came over him, giving him the assurance he needed that everything was going to be okay. This man knew how to have a conversation with God.

One of his comments that day was, "A lot of people say selfish prayers." God may be using that comment to prompt me to write this chapter. I had heard a similar statement from someone else: "You ask, and receive not, because you ask amiss, that you may consume it upon your lusts" (James 4:3).

Prayer is our lifeline to God, open twenty-four hours a day, never busy or overloaded. Sadly, too many people use prayer only as a life preserver, resorted to only when they are in trouble, very much like the roofer sliding off the barn roof who calls, "Lord, help!" About that time, his pants catch on a nail and stop his fall; and he calls back to God, "You don't need to help me after all."

In so many instances today, we have lost the pure joy of conversation and getting to know another person. Instead, we have an agenda. People talk at each other instead of to each other. The host of a radio talk show uses his skills to swing the conversation back to his own point of view. Television debates feature two people with differing opinions, each trying to out-duel the other with words. Nobody wins; the viewer is frustrated, and the show often deteriorates to cheap entertainment.

Often, we follow the same patterns with God. We talk at God because we want something from Him. We do not talk with God for the sheer pleasure of His fellowship.

Prayer is all about having a relationship with God through Jesus Christ. Prayer is communion with God. That union was broken by sin in the Garden of Eden, but can now be restored by the removal of sin through the blood of Christ.

Placing our faith and trust in Christ and communing and fellowshipping with Him through prayer, we are actually eating of the living bread which Jesus talks about in John 6:33. "For the bread of God is he who comes down from heaven and gives life to the world." Jesus is that bread of God. If I stop having communion with God, my spiritual life would slowly die of starvation, just as my physical body would die without nourishment. In the Lord's Prayer, the phrase "Give us this day our daily bread" asks not only for physical nourishment but also spiritual.

So prayer is a vital part of our life in Christ. When we pray and read His Word, we are partaking or eating of the body and blood of Christ. The Lord's Supper, which we observe until He returns, reminds us that we need the blood of Christ to remove our sins until he returns; we need the resurrected Christ as the living Bread to give us life through His Spirit until he returns; and we need each other, symbolized by the act of foot washing until he returns.

In our communion with God, four essential ingredients of a dynamic prayer life give us HOPE.

H *Humility: Recognizing our need of God*

O *Openness: In brokenness and honesty, laying our hearts before Him*

P *Privacy: Giving God our complete attention, shutting out all distractions.*

E *Exchange: Receiving from God what we need for our daily lives.*

In our fellowship with our Father, prayer, praise, worship, and thanksgiving all come gushing up like a spring of water within us because of the life-giving Spirit from Jesus Christ.

A few years ago, I planned to spread pelletized lime on my lawn. At a local feed service, I loaded up my little half-ton trailer with a little more than half a ton of lime. I had just started down the road when a tire blew out. I pulled off on a side road and managed to unhook the trailer.

Driving home, I had no idea how to solve this problem, and I cried out to God for an answer. Throwing a jack and other tools into my truck, I headed back to the trailer. To my amazement, two local farmers waited for me there. One had a skid steer loader and the other had a tractor with a front end loader.

We found that a spring was also broken on the same side as the flat tire.

One farmer sent me to his shed, where I hooked up his big flatbed trailer to my truck. Then they lifted my trailer with their loaders while I backed the flatbed under it.

The plan was a success, and I marveled at the way God works. Nothing is too great or complicated for him.

Many miraculous answers to my prayers have amazed me, but it is the prayers of sweet communion and fellowship with my heavenly Father that sustain and strengthen me day in and day out.

Hebrews 5:7 says, "During the days of Jesus' life on earth, he offered up prayers and petitions with loud cries and tears to the one who could save him from death and he was heard because of his reverent submission." If Jesus himself needed this connection to his Father, how much more I, a sinful being, need this life-giving connection!

The more I learn to know my heavenly Father, the more I realize my need of Him. Communion with God through Jesus Christ really is my daily bread.

CHAPTER 11

Dying to Live

For many people, it takes a whole lifetime—often spent in suffering or hardship—to come to the realization that it's really not what I want, but what God wants.

In His infinite wisdom and knowledge, God created the universe and all the things therein.

In the beginning, you laid the foundations of the earth, and the heavens are the work of your hands (Ps. 102:25).

"Sovereign Lord," they said, "you made the heaven and the earth and the sea and everything in them" (Acts 4:24).

"You are worthy, our Lord and God, to receive glory and honor and power, for you created all things, and by your will they were created and have their being" (Rev. 4:11).

We are not our own, but we are created by God for His purpose, for His honor and for His glory. In the Garden of Gethsemane, Jesus prayed, "not my will but Thine be done." Not *mine*, but *Thine*. That should be our prayer, too.

God demands all of us. The first and most important commandment that God gave to man is to "Love the Lord your God with all your heart and with all your soul and with all your strength and with all your mind." And the second commandment is to "love your neighbor as yourself" (Luke 10:27).

Does this leave any room for ourselves? The answer is no. The Bible says in 1 Corinthians 6:19-20, "You are not your own; you were bought at a price." We are under the ownership and possession of Jesus Christ, who died and paid for our sins with his own blood.

Husbands and wives, you have taken the vow of marriage and now are no longer your own but are joined together as one and have become "one flesh" (Gen. 2:24). So it is with Jesus Christ when we recognize our sinfulness and come to Him. We are no longer our own; we belong to Him.

Compromise is not possible in the Christian life. You are either for Him or against Him, either dead or alive. If you don't surrender your whole life to Him, you really haven't surrendered it at all. It is all or nothing.

Many Christian people live in defeat and struggle with sin all their lives because they have not learned the lesson of dying. You cannot become spiritually alive unless a death takes place. Paul explains this struggle in Romans 7.

> *For I have the desire to do what is good, but I cannot carry it out.*
> *For what I do is not the good I want to do; no, the evil I do not want to do—*
> *this I keep on doing. Now if I do what I do not want to do, it is no longer I who do it, but it is sin living in me that does it.*
> *What a wretched man I am! Who will rescue me from this body of death?*
> *Thanks be to God—through Jesus Christ our Lord! (vv. 18-20, 24-25)*

Romans 8:12-13 says "we have an obligation but it is not to the sinful nature, to live according to it. For if you live according to the sinful nature, you will die; but if *by the*

Spirit you put to death the misdeeds of the body, you will live ..." (emphasis added)

Jesus said in John 12:24-26, "I tell you the truth, unless a kernel of wheat falls to the ground and dies, it remains only a single seed. But if it dies, it produces many seeds. The man who loves his life will lose it, while the man who hates his life in this world will keep it for eternal life. Whoever serves me must follow me; and where I am, my servant also will be."

The rich young man whose story is told in Matthew 19:16-21 was unwilling to give up his life, unwilling to die. Here was a young man who, in today's time, would be described as a boy who loved and obeyed his parents, grew up as the ideal son, took over his father's business, and become very wealthy. Yet Jesus told him to sell his possessions "and give to the poor, and you will have treasure in heaven. Then come, follow me" (verse 21).

But "when the young man heard this, he went away sad, because he had great wealth" (verse 22).

The point of the story is not that it is wrong to have possessions or wealth, but it illustrates what Jesus taught in Matthew 6:19.

> *"Do not store up for yourselves treasures on earth, where moth and rust destroy, and where*

thieves break in and steal.

    But store up for yourselves treasure in heaven..."

(Matthew 6:19-20)

Verse 21 of the Matthew teaching is the key. "For where your treasure is, there your heart will be also."

Our son Chad is a good illustration of giving up one thing that is loved to follow a deeper love. As he made plans to get married, I wanted to give him a gift with a special meaning, a gift from father to son that would be a reminder of my love for him and all the times we spent together creating memories in his growing-up years.

A few weeks before the wedding, I found just the item I was looking for. Chad loved to golf, and here was a wooden, felt-lined box by P. Graham Dunn that held six golf balls. An engraving on the cover showed a golfer swinging a club. I added another engraving that said, FROM DAD TO CHAD, with the date of his wedding. Inside, I put six of Chad's favorite golf balls Pro V1, all number 2s.

I wrapped the gift and stashed it in my truck, waiting for the right time to give it to my son. On the morning of the wedding, I came home and saw that Chad had just finished washing his car and thought this would be the perfect time to give him the gift.

As I handed him the box, I explained that this was a gift from me to him and that the number 2 Pro V1 balls represented his and Sarah's marriage, the two becoming one. Our son was leaving home for a greater love that had won his heart, a love that would bring two lives together to begin one new life.

For a moment, Chad was a little boy again, throwing his arms around his daddy with all the love and emotion being poured out in the biggest embrace I've ever received. We both could do nothing but stand there and weep because words could not express what we felt. What happened in that moment, I will cherish forever. I have said on numerous occasions that I am not rich—but I am very wealthy.

Jesus says in Matthew 10:37, "Anyone who loves his father or mother more than me is not worthy of me; any one who loves his son or daughter more than me is not worthy of me."

Where is your heart? What are your desires? Is your treasure a job or family, wife or grandkids, house or bank account? Or is it Jesus Christ who is most important in your life?

We have come to share in Christ if we hold firmly till the end the confidence we had at first. As

has just been said, "Today, if you hear his voice, do
not harden your hearts as you did in the rebellion"
(Heb. 3:14-15).

We live in the I-generation; everything is about what I
want and what makes me feel good. Too many people try to
use Jesus to accomplish their own purpose in life.

But life really isn't about us at all. It is about the Author
of life, Jesus Christ. It's about dying with Him, so we can live
and let Him accomplish His purpose in our lives.

About the Cover

The cover of this book was designed to symbolize the messages on my heart.

The soil represents the soil of our hearts, and the plow is the word of God (Jesus Christ), that through the power of the Holy Spirit tears open hard and crusty heart soils so that the seed of faith may be sown.

A team of horses reminds us of our new life in Christ, being yoked together with him. The sunrise is like our resurrection with Christ, the dawning of a new day bringing joy, peace, love and a harvest of righteousness.

The connection of two letters by a cross in

the title DYING TO LIVE, carries the message that the I of self has to die on the cross with Christ before true life in Christ can take place in me (Gal. 2:20).

The title also spells Love and Nov., meaning Christ brings love into our lives and November 22, 2011 is forty years since my dad passed away.

The Amish boy represents my Amish heritage.

My name is written in the soil because I am created from the dust of the earth, born to Jacob A. and Orpha Yoder on August 24, 1949.

Dying to Live–Living to Love

Acknowledgments

Thanks to my wife, Cindy, for her love, friendship, and understanding heart. (She is still more mature than I am!) A special thanks to everyone who has said a prayer on my behalf, from my dad, mom, and grandmother to my brothers and sisters and maybe even someone whom I have never met.

I want to thank Elaine Starner, who edited this book. Elaine worked for a local company for many years, but felt God calling her to step out on her own and do freelance writing. Without her obedience to this call, I and many other local writers would probably never have our work published. She has been an inspiration to me and I'm sure to many others, helping us accomplish what otherwise looked like an impossible task. I want to thank her from the bottom of my heart for believing in me to share with others the message I felt God put in my heart.

My thanks to Paul V. Stutzman for inspiring me to write and also thanks to Erika Nofziger for doing the cover photography.

God has called me to be a prayer warrior for Him, and my prayer for you is that God will roll away the stone from the door of your heart and release you from the grave of sin so that the warmth of the love of the resurrected Jesus may shine in your life. My prayer also is that when I meet Jesus face to face, He will allow me to kneel down and kiss His feet for walking with me on this life's journey.

May all who read this book be drawn closer to our loving Savior Jesus Christ.

About the Author

Rob Yoder is a native of Holmes County, Ohio. Growing up on the outskirts of Walnut Creek, he was a teenage rebel who later experienced a revelation that turned his life around forever. He and his wife, Cindy, reside in Apple Creek, Ohio. Together they raised two children and are the proud grandparents of two grandsons. Rob enjoys taking an active role on the prayer team at Fairlawn Mennonite, where he and his wife are members. This is Rob's first book.

I am truly blessed to have a godly earthly father whose love gives me a glimpse of what the love of my Heavenly Father is like. He is one of the most spiritually grounded people I know. His heart is passionate about telling others about the love of Christ and what Christ has done in his life. We are all on this journey of faith together, and our call is to help each other along the way through both the joys and the valleys of life. My father has been an excellent example of this in my own life. He would be the first to admit that he was not and is not the perfect father; but more than anyone else, he has helped shape me into the person in Christ that I am today. For this reason, he is more than just my dad; he is a brother in Christ.

Amber Troyer

86